jokes
to
offend
men

jokes to offend men

Allison Kelley   Danielle Kraese

Kate Herzlin   Ysabel Yates

Illustrations by Millie von Platen

Andrews McMeel
PUBLISHING®

For anyone who could use a little laughter
and catharsis at the end of a long day.

Contents

Introduction

If you're reading this, you probably saw the title of our book and thought it might come in handy. Or maybe you're a man who saw the title and are already offended. Either way, welcome!

We wrote this book because we were tired of watching countless men excuse their bad behavior by insisting that the real problem is our stunning inability to "take a joke."

As four comedy writers, we've grown up hearing that "women aren't funny" and watching popular culture celebrate "comedy" that relies on making people with less power the butt of the joke. We believe that comedy should empower rather than cause harm. And that there's still a lot of ground to cover when it comes to why that chicken crossed the road.

We're not here to offend all men; we're not even here to offend *just* men! These jokes target people who uphold the patriarchy by using their privilege in harmful ways: a doctor insisting that your pain is all in your head, your co-worker Greg taking credit for your work, a politician shutting down polling sites, or the person you live with making you do all the vacuuming because he thinks you're "just better at that stuff!"

If you're tired of being the punchline, or just tired, we hope this book can be a resource to share with someone who needs to hear it, or a pick-me-up after an exhausting day of dealing with all the various "Gregs" in your life.

Jokes to Offend Men at Work Who Don't Actually Do Their Own Work

These will get the job done, and then Greg's job, too.

A man walks into a bar. It's a low one, so he gets a promotion within his first six months on the job.

How can you tell if a woman at the office is cold?

> Three men have already told her, "Actually, it's the perfect temperature for productivity."

What's found across every industry and through every generation but still considered an isolated incident?

> Unwanted male attention.

Why are the men at my job like parrots?

> Because they repeat everything
> I say, poorly.

You make half as much as me but work twice as hard.
You arrive one hour before me and leave one hour after.
In eight months, I'll be your boss. Who am I?

> Chris, the manager's son.

What did the executive say to his
longtime assistant, Jan?

> Resend me that email so that
> it's at the top of my inbox, Jen.

Why are the men in my workplace like jack-in-the-boxes?

> Because it's only a matter of time before they interrupt me.

What do you call a man who just graduated
with half an internship on his résumé?

Hired.

What do you call a woman with a
strong résumé and gray hair?

"Not a culture fit."

What has a mouth that can speak up for you
but an ass he's trying to save?

Your team member Tim who let you
take the blame for his mistake.

Why was the woman told to speak up?

Because the man was never told to shut up.

"I'm an open book," said the CEO actively fighting against pay transparency.

What did the man do with his bonus?

Spend it.

What did everyone else do with their bonuses?

Wait, what bonuses?

Why couldn't the man do his job?

Because he lied on his résumé and no one questioned his credentials.

"I trust my gut on these things," said the man whose gut has hired thirty-four men this year.

Why did the server buy themself a wedding ring?

So male customers would stop asking if they're on the dessert menu.

A woman was in costume at her work Halloween party and no one successfully guessed who she was.

"Isn't that annoying?" asked a coworker.

"No," she replied. "I'm used to having to defend my clothing choices to the men on this team."

What's something everyone can see
but no one wants to touch?

> How uncomfortable Greg is
> making the new intern.

Why did the award-winning chef's restaurant
get shut down?

> An inspection revealed alarming levels
> of toxic masculinity.

Women are so insecure. How insecure are they?

> They need a job, a living wage, and health
> care benefits to make them feel secure.

What do you call a "She-EO" who runs an MLM company?

   Part of the problem.

Why couldn't the women's volleyball team play in shorts instead of bikinis?

   Well, the team called a foul, but the league sided with the male gaze.

A woman was eating a slice of chocolate cake at her desk.

"Must be your time of the month," her coworker commented.

"Yes, and in June it will be your time of the month," she replied. "We celebrate everyone's birthday on this team."

How was Alex able to talk for two minutes without anyone interrupting?

> Turns out their Zoom was frozen and everyone had already moved on.

Why didn't the man ask for a raise?

> He didn't have to ask.

How many conversations with HR does it take to change a bad light bulb?

> Actually, they decided it was best to just move the light bulb to a different department.

What did the tomato want?

A higher spot on the vine.

What happened when she asked?

She was canned.

What did the job candidate ask the male
hiring manager?

"So, do you have any
questions for me?"

What do women and light bulbs have in common?

They both get replaced when
they burn out.

Why didn't the woman climb
the corporate ladder?

> Because she was focused on
> dismantling capitalism rather
> than continuing to perpetuate a
> system of oppression.

What warning will you find on the back of a pill bottle
and at the end of a job interview?

> "Don't take this if you're pregnant or
> thinking about becoming pregnant."

A top-ranking astronaut had just discovered life on Mars. She rushed back to the ship to alert Mission Control.

"I have an urgent message!" she said through the static. "You're going to want to hear this!"

"So do we," said Mission Control. "Your son's school is on the other line."

"My son's school?" she asked. "I've literally been in orbit for years. Have them call my husband. *He's* the emergency contact."

She looked out the window at Earth, which was just a tiny, blue speck in the distance.

"They know. But they said it'd be easier if they just spoke with Mom."

She sighed and said out loud to no one in particular, "Can you believe this shit?"

"Blop blerg blop!" said the Martian sitting next to her. Which translated to, "I heard things were bad on Earth, but yikes!"

What did relish say when mustard blew off the meeting and asked what he missed?

"Ketchup on your own time."

What do moldy strawberries and the egotistical men at my job have in common?

It only takes a few to ruin everything.

What happened when the woman "leaned in"?

She fell over, broke her leg, and her employer called her "a team player" for returning to work the next day because she couldn't afford not to.

Why didn't the company put its parental leave policy in writing?

> Because the policy was: "If you're thinking of becoming a parent, you should just leave."

"Knock knock."

"Who's there?"

"The only one."

"The only one who?"

"The only one who gets corrected in meetings with my all-male team."

What do men and exclamation points
have in common?

> They make you doubt your professionalism,
> and ultimately you don't need as many as
> you think.

What did the pair of jeans say when their boss
called them "sweetie"?

> "That's inpantilizing."

"Paternity leave? Pssh! My father never took time off
work and I turned out fine," said the boss who did not
turn out fine.

Why did the woman think she
was qualified to fly a plane?

> Because she's literally an airline pilot
> with twenty-four years of experience.

Maya's boss opened up so many doors for her and yet
she was no closer to a promotion. How is this possible?

> They were literal doors.

Who benefits when women are forced to perform their
approachability?

> The exclamation point!

"I've earned every dollar I've ever made," said the white man who was paid a dollar for every sixty-three cents a Black woman at his company was paid for doing the same job.

Why was the headless woman always staying late?

> She had to work so much harder
> to get a-head.

Why is Amina "the office mom"?

> Because she always remembers everyone's birthdays and overextends herself to the detriment of her own mental health!

What kind of ball do companies throw
to marginalized job seekers?

A lowball.

If my coworker Greg got a promotion, what did I get?

Assigned to plan Greg's birthday party.
And I barely know Greg.

Why couldn't the woman break the glass ceiling?

Because she was too busy raising the roof.
What? Women can't party?

What advice did the CEO give to his protégé?

> Fake it 'til you have a controlling stake in it and then lay off half your workforce without warning.

The boss called the new father to discuss his parental leave.

"I have bad news," the boss said, "and I have terrible news."

Bracing himself, the man said, "Tell me the bad news first."

"The bad news is that I'm only giving you twenty-four hours of parental leave."

"Oh no," said the man. "What's the terrible news?"

"That I've been trying to call you since yesterday. I need you to come in today."

What's an unhelpful boss's favorite letter?

"K."

What's the difference between a company
and a family?

One can fire you the second your work
becomes unprofitable, the other is
your actual family, and messaging that
conflates the two is exploitative.

"Ladies," the man said, "for some reason I've decided
it's appropriate to refer to a group of people this way in
the workplace. I should interrogate this."

Why was the angle obtuse?

    He kept calling his coworkers acute.

A woman walks into a bar. "Oops, sorry, didn't see you there, bar!" she says reflexively because she's been conditioned to take up as little space as possible.

Jokes to Offend Men Who Won't Contribute to Housework Because You're "Sooo Much Better at It"

You'll feel right at home, except that here, your labor won't be taken for granted.

jokes to *offend* men

Take my long-term live-in partner, for example . . .

> An example that marriage isn't for every-
> one, and that's totally fine! Whatever
> is best to keep your relationship loving,
> healthy, and equitable.

"Honestly, babe, I don't know why you
need to wear so much lipstick," said the man
in full Patriots face paint.

What do men and jars have in common?

> It's exhausting to get them
> to finally open up.

I don't take up much space but I perform a big job. You ignore me, yet I hang on. What am I?

A hand towel. We exist, Greg.

How often should you wash your sheets?

Oh my god, Greg. Google it.

How do you know if someone is wife material?

The same way you know if they're husband material: you check the tag.

Why didn't the man cook dinner?

> Because he had already meal-prepped for the whole week so the lasagna was ready to go!

Who wears the pants in this relationship?

> The legs.

I need a husband like I need a Form 1040A, in that they both can be useful for tax purposes.

I was growing resentful that my partner refused to do his own laundry. One day I decided I'd had enough. "Are you really going to leave me out to dry?" he said, dangling from the clothesline.

This weather is colder than my spouse's meatloaf, which is only cold because it was refrigerated or else it would develop deadly bacteria, so it's best to keep it cold for food safety reasons.

What has a ring but no finger?

> This coffee table, because my roommate claims to know the material so well, it won't stain, he's sure of it.

jokes to *offend* men

What happened when the husband increased
his wife's allowance?

        An allowance? What is she, his child?
        What the fuck?

A woman walks into a barbecue carrying a package
of veggie burgers. She's immediately grilled about her
food choices.

I have a joke about the equitable division of labor,
but I've never met a man who understands it.

What makes men appealing?

When they start a-peeling some potatoes without me having to ask.

An optimist sees a glass that's half-full. A pessimist sees a glass that's half-empty. Greg sees a glass of water that's spilled and does nothing.

What do you call it when a man makes his spouse schedule all his doctors' appointments?

An unhealthy marriage.

How many people does it take
to change a light bulb?

> Two. One person to change it,
> and a man to make them doubt they
> understand the fundamentals of
> "righty-tighty, lefty-loosey."

When company comes over, why is the woman the hostess with the mostest?

> Because her husband's indifference
> is the grossest.

How come the couple moved in together?

> For a variety of reasons, none of which
> need to end in marriage.

"Looks like I'm sleeping on the couch tonight!" the man said to his girlfriend. "And so are you! The bedroom is haunted and the spirits need to be exorcized. I'm sorry this is how you had to find out."

What was the man's defense for not helping his wife write their wedding thank-you cards?

> "Your Honor, her handwriting
> is just better than mine!"

Why did the man forget his husband's birthday?

> He didn't. His husband doesn't like celebrating his birthday. And the man respected that wish.

"My wife has been nagging me to replace this parachute for years," said the man seconds before plummeting to his death.

A woman walks into a barbell—ouch! It had been left in the middle of the hallway again.

"Sorry," her roommate Dan says sincerely. "I really need to be better about pulling my weight."

Jokes to Offend Men You're Expected to Spend the Holidays With, Unfortunately

You'll be thankful for these when your uncle's toast turns into a tirade.

Why did the dad cross the road?

> Because the neighbor called him a chicken
> and he just couldn't let it go.

What's a question that only gets asked
more after it's been answered?

> "When are you going to have a baby?"

What's the right way to brine a turkey?

> Greg has no idea, but that didn't
> stop him from chiming in.

What do daughters and business cards have in common?

> Men are expected to give them
> away at events.

Why do we drink four cups of wine on Passover?

> Because that's one way to get through
> Uncle Larry's tirade on cancel culture.

A woman, her daughter, and the family babysitter
are in a car accident. The woman dies instantly. The
young girl and her babysitter are rushed to the hospital.
The girl needs surgery, but the babysitter is fine. The
doctor tells the babysitter, "It's okay, you can go home."
And the babysitter says, "I can't leave this girl here—
she's my daughter." How is this possible?

> The "babysitter" is her dad.

What do men and pies have in common?

> They both need to go outside
> to cool off.

> They have a dry, crusty exterior.

> There's nothing worse than having
> a bad one thrown in your face.

Sometimes they're sweet, and other times
they're rather unsavory.

> They both try to explain math to me.

I'm expected to serve them during
the holidays.

> They require far too much time
> and labor.

When given the option, I'll always
prefer cake.

What did Greg say to his sister on Mother's Day?

"So, what gift did we get for Mom?"

What did the little "lady killer" grow up to be?

Ted Bundy.

What did Ted Bundy grow up to be?

Played by Zac Efron.

Why did the women get stuck washing all the dishes on Thanksgiving?

The men didn't know they needed help!
Why didn't anyone tell them?

Do you think Santa Claus is real?

> A man who demands you believe in him
> despite no evidence? Sounds real to me!

What's it called when you expect women
to hate carbs?

> Enforcing outdated gender rolls.

"My son loves the ladies!" said the father who won't
buy his five-year-old books with a gay protagonist
because he's "too young for sexuality."

What did my uncle say to my dad
on his birthday last year?

> Nothing; men aren't encouraged to
> communicate.

What did my uncle say to my dad
on his birthday this year?

> A lot because he recently started going
> to therapy and they were finally able to
> open up about their parents' divorce and
> how they both reacted to it differently,
> and, even though they grew apart, they
> ultimately have a shared trauma and
> should schedule more regular phone
> conversations to talk about how they can
> break the cycle and be better fathers to
> their children.

jokes to *offend* men

How many uncles does it take to screw a light bulb?

Just one, and he'll tell you about it in
graphic detail after he's had a few.

I like my men like I like my eggnog: not spoiled.

I like my men like I like my green bean casserole:
not afraid to play a supporting role.

I like my men like I like my beets: not touching
anything on my plate.

I like my men like I like my potatoes: roasted!

I like my men like I like my creamed spinach:
in very small doses.

I like my men like I like my oven: self-cleaning.

I like my men like I like my carrots: I don't like them.

What do Greg's mom and his girlfriend
have in common?

> Both of them are expected
> to mother him.

What do the holiday turkey and my husband
have in common?

> Nice legs.

"Knock knock."

"Who's there?"

"Luke."

"Luke who?"

"Now luke who's talking over me again—Uncle Luke,
who apparently still has more to say!"

jokes to *offend* men

What's the worst part about traveling
to your family reunion?

> Having to help the men unpack their
> emotional baggage when you get there.

What makes this night different
from all other nights?

> Honestly not much, because the men
> still aren't offering to clear the table.

jokes to *offend* men

If a daughter is daddy's little princess, what is a son?

An autonomous king

Able to form his own identity

Daddy's little drinking buddy

Out back helping daddy bury the family dog after a tragic accident

Not infantilized in that way

Next in line to take over the family business

A lady killer, which is a lot to unpack

A chip off the ol' block, and the block is made of outdated gender roles

There's no place like home for the holidays. Which is why I'm staying home this holiday because I've cut off contact with my toxic family.

What did the man do after being introduced to the concept of emotional labor?

Asked his spouse to explain it to him.

What did he say after it was explained?

"Oh, I wasn't listening. Explain it again."

A woman walks into a bar with her date. And her older brother, uncle, and male cousins follow them there, because they still don't respect her autonomy.

Jokes to Offend Men Who Are Currently Explaining Quentin Tarantino to You

You'll find zingers more timeless than whatever sexist movie Greg can't believe you haven't seen.

jokes to *offend* men

How can you tell if a man loves *Manhattan*?

> He may love films in black and white, but
> he considers age of consent a gray area.

Have you heard the one about the Bechdel Test?

> Sorry, I can't answer that. I'm a female
> character in a movie and I'm only allowed
> to talk about men!

What do you say to a man who's explaining
Steven Spielberg's cultural impact to you?

> "You were so preoccupied with whether
> or not you could explain this to me, you
> didn't stop to think if you should."

How many women authors could the man name?

> None, but he could have sworn
> C. S. Lewis was a woman.

Why did the man direct the female
coming-of-age movie?

> They made him an offer
> he could have refused.

Where does *Star Wars* take place?

> A long time ago in a galaxy close enough
> for sexism to still be pervasive, apparently.

jokes to *offend* men

How can you tell if a man has read *Infinite Jest*?

> His text reprimanding you for not
> finishing it has a footnote containing
> a second reprimand for never reading
> *Consider the Lobster*, arguably David Foster
> Wallace's most accessible work.

What do you say to a man who keeps droning on about
the genius of *Taxi Driver*?

> "You talkin' at me?"

Where will you find a man who loves
Jack Kerouac but won't ask for directions?

> *On the Road.*

jokes to *offend* men

How many men does it take to write
a problematic teen movie?

       Just one, plus all the other people who
       never stopped to question the rape scene
       that was played for laughs.

I've watched *The Godfather* three times,
slept through it a fourth time, and still
don't like it. How is that possible?

       According to my roommate, Greg, it's not.
       I'm just not giving it a chance.

What do you call a man who's watched
The Shining a hundred times but has never
seen a film by a non-male director?

       A dull boy.

Why are so many action movies about men needing to "win back" their wives?

>Because it's apparently easier to jump over a volcano or blow up the moon than go to couples therapy.

What do you call it when the media slams
a tennis pro for expressing frustration like
her male counterparts do all the time?

A racket.

What do you say to a man who doesn't
try to explain classic films to you?

"I think this is the beginning
of a beautiful friendship."

Where do you send a man who belittles
you for liking Pixar?

To infinity and beyond.

jokes to *offend* men

After the couple had a big fight, the man got in his car and drove away. Hours later he returned and interrupted his wife's book club to announce: "You complete me." With tears in her eyes, the woman said, "And you completely misunderstood me when I said I wanted a sincere apology instead of an empty platitude in front of all my friends. Please go. I don't find this romantic."

What happened when the director shot a hetero sex scene where the woman *didn't* have a screaming orgasm immediately upon penetration?

Too many men complained that it was unrealistic.

What do you say to a guy who watches
Titanic and empathizes with Cal?

"My heart will go on."

Who are the biggest fans of
strong female characters?

The men who get hired to write them.

What does the media call a male rock star
with a substance use disorder?

Battling demons.

What does the media call a female rock star
with a substance use disorder?

A demon.

jokes to *offend* men

How do you know you're in the
presence of a creative genius?

> He will remind you.

What do men and Netflix have in common?

> They won't stop recommending
> things that I've already watched.

Beauty is in the eye of the beholder.
Unless you're the heroine of a rom-com,
in which case beauty is dependent
on you taking off your glasses.

What do you say to a guy who projects all
of his *Mamma Mia!* issues onto you?

> My, my, I can and will resist ya.

What's a male director's idea of character
growth for the female lead?

> Going from three-inch heels
> to five-inch.

"I haven't cried in twenty years," says the female lead, who's not like other girls.

"You might be the most incredible woman I've ever met," says the male lead. "Tell me more."

"My favorite fruit is bacon!"

"Wow, are you my dream girl?" the man asks, beginning to sweat a little. "Anything else?!"

"I think foreplay is overrated! I prefer to minimize any chance of my having an orgasm by skipping straight to the good stuff: bone-dry penetration!"

"MARRY ME," the man screams, sweat gushing from every one of his pores.

"Well, we've only known each other for two days and have yet to navigate any real-world situations that would indicate whether we are compatible for a long-term, committed relationship. But YES, YES, OF COURSE I WILL! WHEEEEEE!"

Write drunk, edit sober, attempt to write
a dynamic female character for once.

What should you say to someone
who has never seen *Star Wars*?

> "That's totally fine and I'm not
> personally offended."

If a remake is called an "all-female reboot,"
what do you call the original?

> All-male bullshit.

How do we know the male lead is a hero?

He's playing a single dad.

How do we know the female lead is a victim?

She's playing a single mom.

How do we know the supporting character is a villain?

She's playing a stepmom.

Which is the best *Godfather* movie?

You've Got Mail.

A woman walks into a bar. And she topples over it because being clumsy is her defining personality trait in this male-directed rom-com.

Jokes to Offend Men Who Disrespect Mother Nature

Nontoxic material that won't bio-degrade you.

What do men and plastic bags have in common?

Their impact will negatively
affect us for millennia.

Why did the lion spit out the climate change denier?

His views were too hard to digest.

Can you believe only 5 percent of the
ocean floor has been explored?

That's 5 percent more than women's pain.

jokes to *offend* men

What do women and bees have in common?

> Everyone sees that they're busy
> but never offers to help.

If a tree falls in a forest and only a woman
is around to hear it, does it make a sound?

> We'll never know. The male forest ranger
> said it was a "she said, tree said" situation.

"Thunder only happens when it's raining,"
the non-binary person sang.

"Well, actually, rain can evaporate before it
hits the ground even while it's thundering,"
the man sang back.

What do a man's confidence and an
oasis in the desert have in common?

      I know better than to trust it.

What do workplace sexual innuendos and
deforestation have in common?

      They both suck the air out of the room.

What do you do with a handsy chemist?

      Get iridium.

What do men and Pluto have in common?

> They were promoted before we knew
> their credentials.

Their demotion got more attention than
anything a woman has accomplished.

> The more we learned about them, the more
> we realized they didn't deserve their title.

They got too much real estate in my
school textbooks.

> They were both judged by their potential
> and not their accomplishments.

Despite the evidence, people will continue
to defend their position.

How will we know if there's life beyond
our planet?

      When a billionaire finds it, kills it,
      and mounts it on his wall.

jokes to *offend* men

How do you track down a planet killer?

Follow his carbon footprint.

What do women and fossil fuels have in common?

The best strategy is to leave
them both alone, thank you.

What did the rhino say to the businessman on a
hunting trip?

"Please don't kill me in a violent
and selfish attempt to validate
your masculinity!"

A man at the beach walked up to a woman who was alone enjoying a book.

"Hey, what are you reading that's *so* interesting?" he asked. "Some chick lit?"

"Yup," she replied, flipping over her book to show him the cover of *An End to Poultry Farming: The Urgent Threat of the Chicken Industry on Our Environment and Where We Go from Here.*

What do tigers and men have in common?

>Each believes they are endangered, but only one is correct.

Why do we call our planet "Mother" Earth?

> We think its main job is to support life but we don't support it back.

> We won't appreciate all it's done until it's gone.

> Empty statements about its importance stand in for real actions that could actually help.

> We're always expecting it to bring us water.

> We mine it for energy 24/7 and once a year we give it a card.

> Because as long as we assume it's a woman, we'll be happy to keep using it.

When don't the wealthiest 1 percent want to be recognized for their accomplishments?

> When the accomplishment is 10 percent of global emissions.

jokes to *offend* men

What do women and sharks have in common?

> The movies that men make about them
> skew our perception for decades to come.

If Martians live on Mars, what lives on Earth?

> Nothing for very long, at this rate.

Greg is so unhelpful.

How unhelpful is he?

He thinks the scientific method stops after step one:
"Make an observation."

Why is the sun the center of the solar system?

His dad owns the universe.

What do cars and powerful men have in common?

I like to imagine a world that isn't
built solely for them.

A woman walks into a barracuda.
The experience is still less predatory
than walking into a bar.

Jokes to Offend Men You Definitely Didn't Vote For

For all those times you're called "politically correct" because you're correct, politically.

"As the father of a daughter, I vote no on this bill," said the senator. "I don't want my daughter to live in a country where her father's taxes go way up."

What do you get when you put a man
in charge of a crisis?

> A six-figure book deal for a tell-all that recounts how he brilliantly solved the crisis that is very much still ongoing.

A Republican senator walked into a bar graph.
It showed him how many voters he'd need to
disenfranchise to keep his seat.

What was the male politician wearing?

> A suit of some kind? Hard to know—it
> wasn't the focus of several Fox News
> segments for days after the debate.

What do you call a man with multiple credible
sexual misconduct allegations against him?

> Governor, or Justice, or Senator,
> or Mr. President, or . . .

What's the difference between an abortion
and a senator who opposes reproductive rights
on religious grounds?

> One is an affront to all that is holy and
> decent, and the other is an abortion.

The politician is "so dedicated" to equality.

How dedicated is he?

He has the same number of red ties as blue ones.

What do the electrical grid and working
parents have in common?

> They're both under a lot of stress
> and in need of policy-based solutions.

What did the mayor say to the governor?

> "Isn't it cool how neither of us is a man
> even though most people would assume
> we are based on our job titles?"

What do powerful men and the Electoral College have in common?

They're outdated and problematic.

Their interests override what most of us want.

Historically, they've misrepresented their intentions.

Their main function is to keep straight cis white men in power.

They're easily manipulated.

They're protected by our earliest founding documents.

They rely too heavily on their academic credentials.

Nobody really knows what they do all year.

They'll be the downfall of our democracy if we don't do something about it.

Where do babies come from?

> Conservative lawmakers have no clue,
> but that won't stop them from legislating
> away reproductive rights.

The closer the possibility of me seems, the further
away the reality becomes. What am I?

> A woman president.

Why didn't the senator cross the road?

> He hasn't voted to fund that thing
> since the '70s, you actually expect
> him to drive on it?

How did the female politician become "likeable"?

> Wait, you mean there's a way?!
> Please, for god's sake, tell us how!

What do gender equality and the
Leaning Tower of Pisa have in common?

> Efforts to prop it up are too often
> relegated to a photo op.

What do abortions and murder have in common?

> Nothing, so could we please stop
> comparing them?

How can you tell if a female politician
loves her children?

> She'll tell you repeatedly, because if she
> doesn't, she'll be labeled by the press as
> power hungry and coldhearted.

"Wow, look at all those people waiting to vote—that's
democracy at work!" said the Republican incumbent
who shut down all the other polling sites in this
mostly Black and Latinx county.

How many Republican senators does it take
to change a light bulb?

> None. They welcome the return
> of the Dark Ages.

jokes to *offend* men

What do you call a politician who leaves office
after sexually harassing his colleagues?

> In a strong position to
> run again in a few years.

What do student loans and politicians who break
campaign promises have in common?

> They both generate a lot of interest and
> prevent us from moving forward.

I have a joke about clean drinking water, but millions
of Americans still don't have access to it.

"Traditional fowl-mily values are under attack," said the rooster.

"Cluck off," said the chicken.

How can you tell the "pro-life"
politician is lying?

> Because he calls himself "pro-life."

A female politician walks into a bar and orders a round
of drinks.

"I'm sorry, I just can't see myself having a beer with
her," says the man having a beer with her.

Jokes to Offend Men Who Think the #MeToo Movement Has Gone Too Far

For when you're told that affirming your basic human rights is a slippery slope.

jokes to *offend* men

How can you tell if a powerful man
has been "canceled"?

> He'll talk about it on his TV show, write
> about it in his next book, and tweet about
> it to his millions of followers.

Why did the genderqueer person
delete their Facebook?

> They didn't—they just blocked you, Greg.

If a man is playing devil's advocate,
how many hours will he continue to talk
at you if you just smile and nod?

> I don't know yet, ask me when he's done!

jokes to *offend* men

Why did the man cross the road?

> To stop another man from harassing
> someone, which, if you're in a position
> to help, is the right thing to do.

What do a football and a star athlete who
abuses his family have in common?

> There's a whole infrastructure of people
> huddling together, strategizing to protect
> and hold on to them at all costs.

Why wasn't the woman allowed to testify
against her assailant?

> The court decided that her outfit
> spoke for her.

If boys will be boys, what will everyone else be?

> Blamed

> Collateral damage

> Undervalued

> Discussing this in therapy

> Ignored

> Held to a higher standard

> Tired

> Scared to walk home alone at night

> Left to explain why this phrase is problematic

What do you call a man who walks into a bar
and calls "dibs" on an attractive stranger?

> A cab.

jokes to *offend* men

How did the man reply to my joke on Twitter?

With a worse version of it.

How can you tell when you've offended a man?

He goes on a rant about how
you're too easily offended.

What do rape kits and our society's deep-rooted
misogyny have in common?

We've barely begun to process them.

What's it called when a man tells a lewd joke?

"Pushing boundaries."

What's it called when someone else tells a lewd joke?

"Out of bounds."

What do you call it when an abusive man complains about being the victim of a "witch hunt"?

Pure hocus-pocus.

I have a joke about a politician who was accused of unwanted touching, but everyone will probably forget about it by tomorrow.

How can you tell if a man has sisters?

> He'll tweet about it as a way to explain
> why he supports the #MeToo movement.

What do constipated bovines and internet
trolls have in common?

> They're both blocked because of
> their bullshit.

What do you call someone who claims to be a feminist
but doesn't believe that trans women are women?

> A lot of things, but definitely
> not a feminist.

"Women are so emotional,"
said the man who just punched
a hole in the wall.

Why did the woman cross the road?

> Because she suspected she was being
> followed, and the other side of the road
> had more people around. Just another day
> walking home from work!

What's the scariest part of any Halloween party?

> An unprotected drink.

What's the difference between Uranus and someone
who refuses to use your pronouns?

> One only sounds like an asshole,
> and one really is an asshole.

Have you heard the joke about PC culture?

> Yes, it was so funny I forgot to
> performatively laugh, and the guy
> who told it yelled at me.

A woman walks into a bar. And then walks right out
of it. The environment was hostile; it was awful.

Jokes to Offend Men Who Have a Medical Degree in Dismissing Your Pain

You'll laugh so hard it hurts, and then a doctor will say it doesn't.

The more I'm ignored, the more I grow.
The more serious I become, the less
seriously I'm taken. What am I?

> An ovarian cyst.

What do you call a female doctor?

> A doctor.

What do women with chronic pain and
Animal House have in common?

> There are men who still insist
> they're both "hysterical."

What did the ob-gyn say when he denied
his patient a copper IUD?

> "Copper? I hardly know her—or, more
> importantly, her husband, who may
> want kids soon!"

What do you call a pharmacist who refuses
to give you Plan B on "ethical" grounds?

> Unethical!

"You don't look like someone who's chronically ill,"
said the doctor with a sigh.

"And you don't sound like someone who studied
medicine for ten years," said the patient.

A man is feeling sick, so he goes to a walk-in clinic. The doctor introduces herself and asks what's bothering him. Startled, the man says, "Oh, I assumed you were the nurse." The doctor frowns and says, "Sounds serious. Let me send you home with some literature."

Why didn't the ear, nose, and throat doctor treat the nodes on his patient's vocal cords?

Because the nodes made her voice so shrill, he couldn't possibly take her seriously!

What do you call a doctor who won't believe your symptoms unless you lose weight?

A bad doctor.

Why did the ob-gyn sew the expectant
father's mouth shut?

> Because he asked her for
> a "husband stitch."

What's the difference between my doctor
and my insurance company?

> I don't know—they both keep
> rejecting my claims.

Is your womb wandering?

> Well, you better go catch up with
> two thousand years of advancements
> in medicine!

"You've lost weight since your last visit," said the physician, leaning in to read the numbers on the scale. "Whatever you're doing, it's working!"

"I have Crohn's disease," the patient reminded him.

What happened when the woman complained of having a pain in her chest?

She was diagnosed as a pain in the ass.

How did the dermatologist respond when he was reported for harassment?

He performed a mole check.

jokes to *offend* men

What do you call a person who menstruates?

> A person who menstruates.

What's black and white and red all over?

> My polka dot sheets because I'm a
> person who menstruates and that
> happens sometimes.

Why did the chiropractor think he could
cure my scoliosis?

> He knew he wasn't qualified to help,
> but he felt he could take a crack at it.

"On a scale of one to ten, how severe
 is your pain today?"

"I don't know, what number do you need
 to hear to take my pain seriously today?"

Three vampires go out to hunt. The first one
returns dripping with blood and asks for a napkin.
The second one returns dripping in even more
blood and asks for a towel. The third one returns
dripping in the most blood of all and asks for a
tampon—they had leaked through their pants
again because menstrual products are hard
to come by in the wild.

What's more painful than a migraine?

> Your assumption that I'm
> overexaggerating my pain.

What did the doctor give his patient Eddie?

> A diagnosis.

What did the doctor give his patient Edie?

> A lecture.

What is menopause?

> A decline in the body of research
> for something that roughly half
> the population experiences but is
> expected to just deal with.

I had a joke about menstruation,
but it leaked before I could tell it.

A woman in chronic pain went to her doctor to ask about a hysterectomy.

"We don't think that's a good idea," the doctor said.

"Why?" she asked.

"We think you may want to have children one day," the doctor said.

"I do. But my wife plans to carry our child," she replied.

"Well, we think you should keep your options open," the doctor said.

Frustrated, the woman asked, "Why do you keep saying 'we'?"

"I always consult my patients' imaginary male partners about their health care, no matter what their sexuality is." Sighing, he turned to face the coatrack. "Is she always this irrational?"

I had a joke about how common miscarriages are,
but hardly anyone talks about it.

What's shameful, disgusting, recurring, and makes
me want to curl into a ball and moan?

> Our society's attitudes toward periods.

What's more "unbelievable" than giving birth
after thirty-five?

> The fact that people still call it
> a "geriatric pregnancy."

What did the orthopedist who dismissed
my knee pain think of this chapter?

He has a bone to pick with it.

I had a joke about hospital care in the US,
but I'll be paying for it for the rest of my life.

A dermatologist walks into a bar and proceeds to
harass a woman who's trying to quietly read. The
bartender tells her, "Oh, don't worry. He's harmless."
The woman sitting next to her says, "If I may offer a
second opinion? I think you better have that removed."

Jokes to Offend Men Whose Great-Grandfather Founded This School

Required reading for anyone seeking a degree of relief from the patriarchy.

Who's the only person harder to fire than a male
professor with tenure?

> His father, who, incidentally,
> also has tenure.

Why didn't the working mother go
to a four-year college?

> Why don't you mind your own business?

Why did Greg fail his Feminist Theory midterm?

> He hasn't a clue, but he's infuriated
> by the misogyny he's sure he's now
> facing—and even more sure he's
> using that term correctly.

jokes to *offend* men

What did the theoretical physicist say when his colleague told him they were sexually harassed?

"Sorry, but I'm going to need to see some proof."

What did the teacher call the male student who raised his hand a lot, even when he didn't know the answer?

Ambitious! Confident! A star student!

What did the teacher call everyone else in class?

I don't know what he called them, but he certainly didn't call *on* them!

What do you say to a teacher with a gender bias?

Bye, ass.

jokes to *offend* men

What's the etymology of "sexism"?

> Something a freshman will gladly
> explain to me, despite me being
> his teaching assistant.

What do high school girls and Scotch have in common?

> Too many men think once they've
> aged sixteen years, they're mature
> enough to consume.

What's another way to say, "Boys just mature
more slowly than girls"?

> "Boys just face fewer consequences
> than girls. Get used to it!"

Did you hear about the writing workshop
with just men?

> It disbanded after one meeting because
> they all agreed their writing was perfect.

There was once a college professor who had a long and
impressive career. Her brilliance knew no bounds. But
one mystery forever plagued her. What was it?

> Why so many men pronounced the
> "Dr." in front of her name as "Ms."

What kind of pasta can get a high school student
suspended?

> Spaghetti straps.

I was designed to hold things, but I have space for nothing. What am I?

A decorative pocket on a pair of girls' jeans.

How did Greg graduate from college so early?

By always taking other people's credit.

"Knock knock."

"Who's there?"

"Izzy."

"Izzy who?"

"Izzy an expert on the subject, or is he just speaking louder than everyone else?"

What kind of playing did the school encourage girls to do?

Downplaying their accomplishments.

"You can't wear that tank top, it's distracting,"
says the teacher who's distracting the class by
sexualizing a seventh grader's body.

If boys get to come of age,
what do girls get to do?

      Age.

What determines whether a discipline
is a soft or hard science?

      The percentage of women
      who take part in it, apparently.

Why did the pencil leave the pen?

> After years of being treated like his
> number two, she realized she could no
> longer put up with being lead on; it was
> time to write her own story.

What might you tell the professor who insists
it's grammatically incorrect to refer to a person's
pronouns as a singular "they"?

> That it's ethically incorrect for them
> to be teaching.

What's hack and white and dead all over?

> My high school's reading curriculum.

Two roads diverged in a yellow wood and I took
the one more traveled because I'm a woman driving
alone at night.

Why did the frat brother cross the road?

> Because that night, while staring at his
> empty beer, he looked around at the
> misogynistic rituals surrounding him and
> he decided this wasn't how he wanted to
> spend his college years. So he refilled his
> red cup for the last time and walked out,
> boldly going Solo.

A woman walks into a bar . . . sorry, a barre class, and
you shouldn't make fun of her for enjoying challenging
aerobics.

Jokes to Offend Men Who Refuse to Believe You're Not Interested in Them

Smile at these if you want to,
but no one will demand it.

Why did the AirPods get along so well?

> They both had an understanding that they were just buds, and neither felt like they were owed more than that.

Why did the woman accept the first proposal she received?

> It was a proposal to move in with her friends and live in platonic bliss.

When is it okay to question a woman?

> When you're on a date. Please, I beg of you, ask me *something*!

"Knock knock."

"Who's there?"

"Greg."

"Greg who?"

"Greg who? Wow, no one's ever asked me
that before. Who am I really? There's so much to
explore! I will now spend the next half hour of our
date talking about myself—don't interrupt."

How do you make a woman on a dating app
send you nudes?

You don't.

jokes to *offend* men

Which came first: the chicken or the egg?

> That's beside the point. They were both
> excellent communicators who checked in
> with each other to make sure they were
> equally satisfied.

Why did the SAT tutor's new love interest dump him?

> Because he refused to get tested.

What do my Tinder messages have
in common with a horse?

> They're both filled with mostly "hey"
> and quickly lead to shit.

Two women and a man were hanging out at the bar. They each chose a song to play on the jukebox.

When the first woman's song came on, she started crying. "This song always reminds me of my grandma. She was the best. I miss her," she said.

When the second woman's song came on, she too started crying. "This song always reminds me of my dad. He taught me everything I know. I wish he were still around."

When the man's song came on, he immediately burst into tears. The women looked at him strangely.

"'Who Let the Dogs Out' makes you emotional?" they said.

"No, but seeing you both openly express your grief made me realize how little I've been able to do the same."

"There are plenty of fish in the sea,"
said the Tinder employee.

"I'm afraid not," said the marine biologist.
"The straight men caught them all for
their profile pics."

I have a joke about unsolicited dick pics, but I've never met a woman who actually likes it.

A man reaches across the table for a check, but it's not the bill. What is it?

> His phone, so he can check Wikipedia for the accuracy of something his date said.

What happened to the man who expected the women in his life to manage his calendar?

> He had a hard time finding a date.

"So, what? You just don't like men?" said the man.

"Yes," said the woman.

How do you increase the chances of a woman smiling?

Don't ask.

What do you do with a man who won't accept
that you just don't like him that way?

Put him in the we're-no-longer-friends zone.

When is it okay to approach a woman in a dark alley?

> When she's on your bowling team and
> you're congratulating her on another strike.

What do you say if a man tries to order for you?

> "I'll have what *I'm* having—an order
> I'm capable of placing for myself!"

What's worse than a man using a first date
as a therapy session?

> He didn't even offer to co-pay.

jokes to *offend* men

"I'd like to ask for your daughter's hand in marriage," the man said.

"Honestly, that sounds like it's between you and her hand," the father said.

If the man pays for the meal, should you put out?

> Sure, put out your hand
> and give that man a high five!

My last boyfriend was so crazy.

How crazy was he?

Actually, I don't know—I'm not a licensed medical professional, so I shouldn't be diagnosing a person's mental health. And either way, "crazy" is a pejorative that we as a society should eliminate from our lexicon.

Why was the zombie surprised when the ghost
ordered a whiskey?

> He didn't think she could handle
> her booOOoos.

Why did the pickup artist eat breakfast alone?

> Because no one cared for his rotten neggs.

"I wish you could see how beautiful you really are,"
the man said.

"And I wish you would give me back my glasses,"
said the woman. "I can't see anything."

"Here," said the man I'd just met, holding out his phone to me. "Give me your number."

I studied it for a moment, trying to think of the right response.

"Fifty dollars," I said. "It's a pretty old model and has some obvious wear and tear."

"That's a fair deal," he said, taking my payment and then walking out of my life forever—a true Craigslist success story.

A man walks into a bar. He has a drink, respects the boundaries of everyone there, and politely leaves . . . nice!

Jokes to Offend Even More Men

You can keep these in your back pocket (unless it's purely decorative).

jokes to *offend* men

What's harder to look at than a Picasso?

> His well-documented history of misogyny.

What did the dinosaur say to the caveman?

> Nothing, because they lived millennia
> apart—but that won't stop Grog from lying
> about how he bravely slayed a dinosaur
> this morning (classic Grog).

What did the statue of a man
say to the statue of a woman?

> What statue of a woman?

Did you hear the one about the prince
who needed saving?

> Of course you didn't. Men's vulnerability
> is vastly underreported.

What did the male woolly mammoth say
to the female woolly mammoth?

> "Can you be less woolly?"

Why did the chicken cross the road?

> To get to the well-lit side.

Why couldn't the toadstool take a seat?

The fungi had spread out and
he didn't leave her mushroom.

A woman is in distress when a knight in shining armor shows up. "Oh, thank goodness you're here," she exclaims. "I'm having trouble polishing my Olympic gold medals. Got any tips?"

Why are there so few female astronauts?

Men feel threatened when women take up space.

How many women does it take to change a tire?

Just one, and it'll be fast because there are no men around to question her abilities.

I have a joke about car crash safety, but it's only been tested for the "average" man.

How can you tell if two ducks have an equitable relationship?

> They have no problem sharing the bill.

Why did the waffle decide to go to therapy?

> So he could leggo his fragile male Eggo!

"Face it, dude, she's out of our league," said the man.

"True," said the other man. "Twenty thousand leagues, to be exact. But we have to bring the captain and her stranded submarine crew back to shore safely."

What's a manspreader's favorite button on the keyboard?

The space bar.

What time is it when a man asks your foot size?

Time to move your seat.

Why did the duck cross the road?

> You don't have to be a chicken to leave a situation that's not right for you.

Three women went to see a mechanic for an oil change. They were spoken to respectfully, charged a fair price, and not pressured into getting anything they didn't need. How is this possible?

> They were on each other's shoulders, wearing a trench coat, pretending to be a very tall man.

"I'm an archeologist. Want to bone?" said the man to the stranger at the bar.

"I'm an archeologist too," the stranger replied. "But I'm not digging it."

What do you say to a dinosaur who won't shut up about the size of his horns?

Tricera*stop*.

"Why buy the cow when you can get the milk for free?"

Because you're asking that question and now you must pay.

What happened when the woman turned forty?

Everyone told her she looked great (for forty).

The chicken was running around with her head cut off. "Calm down," the rooster said. "It's not that serious."

That girl is so cool.

How cool is she?

Every time she walks into a room, people say, "You look cold."

"Knock knock."

"Who's there?"

"Woody."

"Woody who?"

"Woody still be explaining how to make an old-fashioned if he knew that I'm the bartender here?" (Yes—yes, he would.)

"Oh man, I love a good cat fight," the man said, watching two feral cats brawling in the alley behind his house.

Why did the chicken cross the road?

> The rooster has no idea but pledged to launch a full investigation into why so many chickens are flying the coop.

"That's not very ladylike," said the man who knows nothing about what ladies like.

What did the man ask the banana?

    That's ridiculous, men don't ask questions.

A woman walked into a bra. The design was so unnecessarily complicated this was the only way she could get it on.

Acknowledgments

The four of us would like to thank our wonderful agent, Saba Sulaiman, for always believing in this project, for seeing and supporting our vision from day one, and for answering our calls when you didn't even have cell reception (wait . . . how did you do that?). To our savvy and thoughtful editor, Allison Adler, thank you for taking a chance on four first-time authors. And to the whole amazing team at Andrews McMeel Publishing, including Julie Barnes, Madison Schultz, Julie Skalla, Danys Mares, and Dave Shaw, thank you for making this book a reality.

Thank you to our talented illustrator, Millie von Platen, for bringing a delightfully absurd new dimension to our jokes (we will never look at aliens the same way again).

Thanks to Caitlin Kunkel for your trusted guidance and advice through the years. Literally, where would humor and satire be without you?

We're so grateful to the many people who helped us in the process of proposing and writing this book, especially Julie Vick, Ali Solomon, Janine Annett, Jennie Egerdie, Ginny Hogan, Emily Flake, Brian Boone, Sasha Stewart, Elissa Bassist, Andie Villanueva, and Erica Carras.

Thank you to Chris Monks and McSweeney's Internet Tendency for publishing the original piece that inspired this book, and for supporting new voices and giving us a platform to share our words.

And to the humor and satire community of writers and editors: we're endlessly thankful for how much you've shown up for us.

And to everyone who read and shared the piece that started it all: Thank you for making us feel less alone and laughing along with us.

Allison:

I've had the pleasure of surrounding myself with some very funny, kind, and patient people in my life. It's because of them that I was able to write this book.

Thank you to my earliest comedic influences and supporters: My parents and brother for teaching me to find the humorous silver lining in any situation and encouraging me to write about it. And my oldest friends who put up with my foolishness at sleepovers and to this day; it's your fault I'm like this.

I've shared many jokes with co-workers over the years and I want to thank them all for making the work days infinitely better. To my writing groups in Chicago and New York, thank you for making me a stronger writer and convincing me I had something to say.

Lastly, thank you to my husband, Jeff, for believing in me, championing my weirdness, and always finding a way to make me laugh.

Danielle:

I don't know where I'd be without the medley of people who encouraged my writing over the years (probably still trying to break through in my second-choice profession of marine biologist soccer star ice cream scooper). Thank you to the teachers and editors who guided and believed in me, and to my writing cohorts and note swappers who help make my stuff better and inspire me with theirs.

I want to thank the long-time friends who've always laughed with and at me (even when it resulted in withering looks from teachers, coaches, or bosses).

Endless gratitude to my family for always surrounding me with ear-piercing laughter and being a willing audience to my earliest attempts at humor. And thanks especially to my parents for the unwavering encouragement and love, and to my sister for sharing my weird sense of humor and being my original comedy partner.

And finally, to my husband, who makes me laugh the hardest and enables me to be my goofiest: My contributions to this book wouldn't have been possible without you. Thanks for feeding me, supporting me, and setting up your fold-away baby desk for me, all so I could devote countless hours to writing jokes about how terrible men are.

Kate:

With my apologies to my childhood self who swore she would one day fill a section like this with "people I don't thank because you didn't help me at all"; I'll instead thank those who helped very much, including those who helped me grow as a writer and person in young playwrights festivals, college writing workshops, and comedy writing classes.

Thanks also to those who more literally helped me get here at the Cancer Center for Kids—especially my pediatric oncologist, who is still the funniest person I've ever met (sorry to my co-writers).

I want to thank the many people who gave me invaluable advice in the process of pitching and writing this book, with thanks especially to my writing mentors in Philly, New York, and Northampton, and to the absurdly talented people in my writers groups. I also want to express my gratitude to the wonderful people in my life who have taken the time to share their insights with me on accessibility, intersectionality, and experiences beyond my own. Among the many teachers and mentors who I'm forever indebted to, a special shout-out to high school English teachers—those who specifically taught me, and also all of them, just like, in general.

Finally, thanks to my parents, my sister, my family, and my friends who have guided me, supported me, and shown up for me. I'll always be grateful to Grandma Evie and Grandpa Stan for teaching me the Yiddish jokes that were my greatest lesson in comedic timing and made life a bit easier. The biggest thanks to my husband, Ben, whose room-filling laugh I'm really after here; for loving me, believing in me, and being the one man I least hope to offend.

Ysabel:

Thank you to my partner, Juan, for always believing in me, supporting me, and setting up my technology for me. Thank you to my writing group, especially my fellow humor scientist Kerry Elson, and to everyone who has ever read one of my shitty first drafts. Thank you to Audra Klair for all your love and support and for showing me what it means to go after your goals. I don't know where I'd be without you. Thank you to Alex Franco for all the teatimes over the years—your tenacity, humor, and creativity inspires me to keep going. And thank you to everyone in the humor writing community. You all are the most supportive, kind, hilarious, and creative group of people, and I am incredibly grateful to have found my way here.

About the Authors

Allison Kelley, Danielle Kraese, Kate Herzlin, and Ysabel Yates are humor and satire writers based in New York. Their work has been featured in such publications as the *New York Times*, the *New Yorker*, *Reductress*, and *McSweeney's Internet Tendency*.

Andrews McMeel Publishing
a division of Andrews McMeel Universal
1130 Walnut Street, Kansas City, Missouri 64106

www.andrewsmcmeel.com

22 23 24 25 26 RR2 10 9 8 7 6 5 4 3 2 1

ISBN: 978-1-5248-7219-9

Library of Congress Control Number: 2022940942

Editor: Allison Adler
Art Director: Julie Barnes
Production Editor: Dave Shaw
Production Manager: Julie Skalla

ATTENTION: SCHOOLS AND BUSINESSES
Andrews McMeel books are available at quantity discounts with bulk purchase for educational, business, or sales promotional use. For information, please e-mail the Andrews McMeel Publishing Special Sales Department: specialsales@amuniversal.com.